River Nocturne

poems by

Z.G. Tomaszewski

Finishing Line Press
Georgetown, Kentucky

River Nocturne

Copyright © 2018 by Z.G. Tomaszewski
ISBN 978-1-63534-563-6 First Edition
All rights reserved under International and Pan-American Copyright Conventions. No part of this book may be reproduced in any manner whatsoever without written permission from the publisher, except in the case of brief quotations embodied in critical articles and reviews.

ACKNOWLEDGMENTS

Several of these poems previously appeared in various magazines, thanks to those attentive and empathetic editors for their readership:

Empty Mirror: "Dreaming The River"
Portland Review: "Roadkill"
RHINO: "Chronicle"
STAND: "Voyaging"
The Stony Thursday Book: "A Woman Longhaired and Naked Riding"
Talking River: "Consciousness"
Terrain.org: "Cross-hatch"

"Early Magic" won 1st place in the Dyer-Ives Poetry Competition, judged by Oliver de la Paz and published in *Voices*.

"Cross-hatch" appeared as a limited edition broadside thanks to the people at the Kalamazoo Book Arts Center and their Poets in Print reading series.

Publisher: Leah Maines
Editor: Christen Kincaid
Cover Art: Jeff Kraus
Author Photo: Whalen and Shimmin
Cover Design: Jenn Meade

Printed in the USA on acid-free paper.
Order online: www.finishinglinepress.com

Author inquiries and mail orders:
Finishing Line Press
P. O. Box 1626
Georgetown, Kentucky 40324
U. S. A.

Table of Contents

Roadkill 1

Waking Dream 2

Insomniac Poet Reads James Wright 3

Chronicle 4

Voyaging 5

A Woman Longhaired and Naked 7

Some Character Types of the Internal Dream-like Novel 8

Claiming 11

Traveler 12

Spell 14

Early Magic 16

Voice 17

Consciousness 18

Cross-hatch 19

Sundial 20

A Day at Large 21

Riverside 22

Dreaming the River 23

Elegy on How to Return 26

Notes

As the day goes my mind keeps turning
toward you, making the curve
it loves, going away only to return.
Soon now the dark will come, and I
will go again into the unknown country.
Too long I have been dull and spare
as a winter stem, that bears at last
the warm opening flower of new desire.
It is the return of possibility,
the power to cast away from the known,
that warms me as I turn and look
toward the woods and the distant hills.
The past, the day's dead light, grows
heavy, turning toward new dawn. Again
I can imagine the joyous departure,
the opening of the dark, the going in.

        Wendell Berry
        Section II of "Inland Passages," The Lover,
        The Country of Marriage

Roadkill

And when she's frightened, your daughter,
you turn the light on and begin telling her
about the origin of shadows, which makes you
think of your own childhood and its sleepless nights.
As you keep to the story of how
one little girl danced among constellations
you notice your daughter start to lull off
and hope she pivots peaceful into the other realm,
still considering your own sleep,
wondering when it may come.

Once she's fallen asleep you leave her
to return to the road which holds
the carcass of a coyote. Standing above it,
the smell, river in its skin, its eyes with dried
blood and flies and a mouth open mid-howl—
you want to bury the roadkill, so you unfold the road
and lower the stiff musculature of the past—
all those sensations returning primal—
your daughter dancing along Orion's belt,
stars spiraling off, sifting down like snow,
the wind weaving the fallen to the ground.

Waking Dream

1.

At the end of the film they're calling her name.
She keeps walking.
The credits roll.

Somewhere in another movie
a dog barks,
at the same time
in the theatre
a quarter falls from someone's pocket.

The sky coughs up a cloud.

2.

I catch sight of my childhood house in the rain:
a dirt road coasts through it, I ride right in.
Someone else's family is there, I wave.

On my bicycle I keep gliding, pass a house, then another,
one of them has a roof being repaired.

Insomniac Poet Reads James Wright

Awake, again, another
god-awful night.

How come this hospital
has no running water?

There's an owl here and my head
swivels on a worthless stem.

Once, I heard the low, sweet
sorrowful notes of an oboe drowning

downstream, a carousel of clouds
and fractured light, my mother

and father leaving their love,
an abandoned house upstream.

The owl turns his head.
A dying flower

barely opens.
Step back from the river.

The alarm sounds, my parents
across the river howl at the moon—

or each other.

Chronicle

Wind is voice unshaped.
Every window ready to be a self-portrait.

You draw back your hand from god's pocket
to find the entrance stone.

We share the author's vision:
a cat goes missing and the religious search begins.

How squandering light leaves us
a shadow without substance.

A bald woman loses
her hat and a moth lands there.

History as incomplete
as a clock under water.

A pipe begins leaking
along a dark, narrow hallway,

a cane at the other end.
The cat chases the moth

like slow undivided time.
And the woman whose life I do not understand

falls asleep on a bed of hats
while the old man approaches her window.

Voyaging

What happens is nothing happens.
What happens is we fall so far
Into a sleep so manifold,
Not even nightfall, whose gold we are, can find us.

I.

A generous crop of corn shucked out on the field.
Wind raking the maize, pushing at my back and brushing
million-year-old-dust against my face.

There was an old man's voice. He was the local earth-dweller.
I felt my body quicken towards him. Water over stone.

II.

What the Indian said of the road I'm to travel:
    Not many will pass this way.

The voice came from the dream a cloud might contain,
    released when the sun shakes its feathered hat.

The voice textured with bone
contains the story's preface:

It was laid out before me.
I could choose to travel it or not.

Yet I was already passing through.

IV.

While there are no stars, only
ghosts of graying clouds
shaded blue with absence,
millions of silver
mallets strike the tonal surface.

V.

The old man with a feather beard makes marimbas from trees. Already a cricketing timbre, branches clack like drumsticks overlapping in Anathallo's "Genesserat." His weathered hands hold the hollow bones of bird nests, horizon gaining as eggshell clouds crack and yolks slide Dali-style down the sky's face.
  A widow broomcorn sweeps the news gathered yesterday by her front door—dust so fine it whispers through the screen, not even light can touch it. If we could see what the widow sees: that dusk rising into a murmur of birds and blossoming galaxies; if we could see what she sees maybe our loneliness would not leave us to write our names in the sand.
  The stick is a bone is the old man's mallet and the widow's broom handle. The dog sidetracks his interest like a child and with wand in mouth barks at the sky—a spell: substitutes sun for moon.

VI.

Night sewn by the Indian hands of my ancestors' oldest
memories.
Ghost garments: the fog my headlights unfasten
from an Alaskan fabric.

The gray echo of a hand ripples
as the wave of my past
reduces to a blind shimmer.

A Woman Longhaired and Naked

Riding a horse unsaddled and satin black
far into the forest, but from behind
(and it's always that way replayed):

a portrait of the going, focal point shrinking
as they become the transcendent line.
Part of him must be

the cricket's reverb, a shape transfigured
by the willow's braid,
a freckle of wind on the waterskin.

Nearsighted, he lacks the focus
to bring the horse with the woman
out from the woods—
to ask, *why am I here?*
—and the fabric of language frays

like a rope made of water,
rivulets of silk rolling off, each drop
a knot, unlooped and spooling out.

Some Character Types of the Internal Dream-like Novel

The willow
unfolds its barked skin
and as it opens
invites me further into

a world where cats talk in riddles,
discarded bags of chips serve
as P.O. boxes for mail the clock-like
birds receive,
a world of interlocking marimbas and
overlapping pan flutes—

hoot hoot, who are you?
from the Indian owl who spins rhythms
of hollowed vowels
while its tremolo head spikes up
into orbs of feathers as the wind
choreographs a dance—

I like language when it's peeled apart
and put back together.
The fence of civilization—

the white toothpicks of our shared
American dream, the twigs gnarled
between some potato-shaped man's jaw—

not my father
thinking about his possessions,
what he owns and owes
and how to retire with enough days
to make it all right, the scale needing
to balance—

how measuring a wheel of cheese
in the Polish neighborhood of my past
was handled in the center of town so
whoever wanted to witness could watch,
while all the mice lie in wait—

they built alleys to bring the cats out
and soon a shelf was nailed
to the membrane of the future where
cans of paint were put to color
the black and white of our childhood—

and yesterday
an oboe was reported missing
from the museum and I know
I saw it there in the river
moving along at its leisure—
breathing occasionally—
a single bubble rising and then
an eddy and the vessel pulled under
swirling in the manifold before
sounding out a little but deeply felt
melancholy note—

but the willow whose branch
reaches in to my window,
whose leaves look
like my family's fingers and whose leaning
against the wind reminds me of
how birds counter air to accept gravity—
how surrendering gives us the most
ancient and lively force—

the heart lifting not because of love
but because of Sound
and how she waltzes on,
nearly weightless, away from
the empty grip of the void, and gains weight
with each instrument she passes through—
stitching a thin thread of melody
in each pattern she moves among—

I hear every decibel of the river—
the oboe of the soul—
the tremolo hello of the owl and his asking
me to die, to join him in the next dance—

and if I'm one of the mice
then I must know
how to give myself over—
the Buddhist cat not stealing itself towards me
but not trying to save me either—

so I peel the word back
to feel its percussion and become
what I already was—

a single missing chord
from the entire orchestra being compressed
into the perfection of dissonance.

Claiming

> *I touch the water, and the water*
> *knows your name. I fill my hand with fallen stars*
> *and signal from the river.*

The oar of my canoe widens
as an old Indian song
wakes from hibernation.

There are no words
for the peeling back
of shore, no names
we know by which to call it—

waves vibrating,
stirring hardwood,
the hull of a boat arched
like a turtle's head,

and the grace of a body
nearly weightless in water;
the day unnumbered and
moving toward evening

where a heron wades,
afternoon's heaviness lifts,
and the turtle slips into
the cool night suit of water.

It swims in my eyes:
the claiming song,
surfaced and
chanting.

Traveler

Home is a collection of details,
not every detail from the place we are born.

*Like the river we go out from the source
glean, return, deposit.*

When I reach the delta…
When I touch the confluence…

The running on and on of the current…

*The minerals we need are deep in us, but
we must touch the earth time and again*

Someone once said, "You know you're close
by how far you've come."

*to know and be
reminded. To touch the earth's every fold,*

The brackish waters of my past
have tributaries I've tried to follow
but my heart is downstream,
my waders own holes.

When the ferryman finds me and says little
about my boat or lack of boat
and says nothing of my waders
then I know what's he's really saying.

I take my clothes off and listen
to the skin of the matter…

each scar—the rivering on, moving over and within.

The ferryman humming, someone whispering.

You know you're close…
"How far you've come."

Spell

Picasso-blue light of solstice dawn

    *

The woodsman starts by telling me there's new beaver activity

    *

As I grow older I appreciate more and more geese united and flying north

    *

I want to share it with you the whole sky one soft dissolving fragment at a time

    *

I would have made a tapestry from the river using yesterday's rain to give the gods one moment of equilibrium

    *

Blackbird with red wings balanced on a reed

    *

Hawk takes the whole weight of itself and drops from sky

    *

They say you can always come back

    *

Lay me down beneath the heron's dusky wingspan

*

Such darkness we're running towards

Early Magic

An empty whiskey glass greets me as a mirror of night, multiple Saturns swirling all over the universe, when I reach for the switch the bulb flickers and each planet finds its place. I'm sitting with a half cup of coffee juggling July 1989 and the roads of Grand Rapids. Yesterday a bag slung over my left shoulder, right arm out, hand-cocked and thumbing the pages of wind. Eventually I hitch on with a grandfather who drives me to the end of this dimension, bottle drying out, and when the door clunks shut and gravel groans I see in the billow of exhaust fumes a name sputtered in cursive. This time identity finds me in the split instant of dust sieved down from broken stars, as fog hovering a pond and a winged creature threading through the owly mist, as lipstick on cigarette butts and an ashtray of snuffed kisses, the sky smoking American Spirits and puffing out clouds, the tilted alcohol and loose talk that pours from it. I was listening to that feeling in my gut and danced all the way into darkness and pulled the curtain of darkness down and stomped the darkness under my feet and the moon came through begging I take her hand and I reached and leaned in and with fingers overlapping we began to spin. Then all those stars shuffled and I fell fast, while a dog came walking by with its leash around the sun. I flipped the whiskey switch and light poured into the room. The dog barks. Later, as in now, the early magic comes spiraling off the coffee spelling the same name grandpa's rusty muffler coughed up.

Voice

One morning I stepped out of…
I stepped into… the haze…

There was a willow… My grandma…

I heard her voice…
It wasn't just a voice…

There were so many textures in the wind…
I could feel the elements…

I won't ever forget it…
It's been on my mind…
I don't know how to tell you…

The sky did this thing…
The willow…
Sunlight like fog…
The wind's pregnant sigh…
A curtain dissolved…
A breath made visible…

I'll never forget what she said…
I'll wait my whole life for it to come true…

One morning I stepped out of…
I entered the haze…
A voice branching toward me…
Roundness hollowed out…
The shout growing…
A dozen mirrors…

Everything… The truth… Wrinkling…

One morning…

Consciousness

Our Piper swoops down
over a stitch of the river
spooking up ducks and
one muskrat stirring snow
along the banks, edging
the meadow, then pulls high
trimming the treetops as
we skim clouds and forget
our names in the crown
of the high-speed instant,
hearing the rough and
tumble air jamming against
the engine while a huddle
of deer lift ears and twitch,
a fox visible by its
wicking tail, denning
down, the Earth folds
under, ridgeline wavering
blue/purple/black/auburn
and now a house flares out
alone in a field, the sheltered
wheat, horses snorts of cold
memories, the landing
coming closer, the plane
altering, river brimming,
ground beating, the tube-
and-rag of the body, fallen.

Cross-hatch

I reach the gap—
the place between rivers,
rivering all day through underbrush
of blackberry, sky folding over
its gauze, and just now
cranes pull through a waxing sun,
net their feathers as a degree of glimmer
edges pupils—I see the shape of
my childhood, breast molting, a memory
shedding facts: my brother
in the hospital bed beside me,
post-surgery, one-organ-less later
and stitches to keep skin from pulling
apart, but the needle—opening
an eye to the piercing light,
the cross-hatch, image-burn,
the way the cranes' wake is a scar
healing, how they cast and break
the spell of their arrival, and here,
the wheat cheering up, softening,
and the river, that place between rivers,
the gap

    my brother eating blackberries.

Sundial

> *Maybe our river, dreaming out loud,*
> *folds story and forgetting*

Lilacs. A junebug entering oblivion. Getting lost
in Montana flats, mountains cutting sky down.
Horse-tied-to-a-stone Browning. Piss into a discarded tire.
Spit. Smell the sage.

I take the pipe from Moose Woman's reach and puff twice.
She smiles then disappears. The undecided sky pitches
a few horseshoes of rain then withholds. I'm left with a feeling
I felt before, like when I shared stories and a joint
with the old bearded man under the bridge while
unreasonably close a kingfisher rattled and splunked into
the Grand River, surfacing with proof of its hunger and accuracy.

Only one arm on my wristwatch works and it's the hour hand
so I tell time like a sundial not once knowing the minute.

When Moose Woman reappears I offer a fistful of dirt
I've been milling in my palm ever since I placed the pipe down—
a dust of galaxies sifted through fingers of time.
I step into her long hair of willow braids, a lilac
dreaded in and junebugs jitter- and weaving.

Maybe I become a synapse: a minnow swimming, darting
back and forth. Maybe I'm a groove in the tire's tread,
maybe her hair is a nebula of kingfisher feathers, the old
man's beard, the metallic surface of a river in a different state
carrying the city's weight in its name, while a horse drags
stone—sagebrush furrowed and smoky.

A Day at Large

> *And night is a river bridging*
> *the speaking and the listening banks*

I follow the unfinished bridge,
take water's hand
to where waves
haul in the bending tree canopy and
broken peaks of mountains.

Radio poles send burnt signals:
ghost trees from the fire a few years ago.

A loon's voice rolls over the river,
its tremolo widening with the water's reverb
and the gulching oar's vibrato against Kintla's
mountain aria, clouds all pizzicato and
the bowed cello of my heart.

Most weeks: a few notes here and others
there. Sometimes, asleep,
the day's missing chords sound.

When I wake to record them
they fade fast and I become nocturnal,
waiting, looking at the small pools
of light in the dark sky, studying
the moving curtain of shadows.

To be called back by the voice of the loon.
To nest in her feathers and feel her
heart chamber resonate as the song paddles
across the water.

Am I missed or missing
as everything enters me?

Like the renegade out from the asylum,
where, to what, do I stand facing,
at large in this world?

Riverside

Some days I want to fill my coat
      with stones.

Some days I fill my coat with stones
      but when I arrive at the river

I take from my past the stones
      and hurl that heaviness from me.

I watch what weighed me filter
      light through my pockets.

I walk away with stones of dusk
      between fingers.

Some nights I walk along the river
      leave part of me there—

Then dawn and I bring some of that world
      back, coat soaked, the stoneful river.

Dreaming The River

Every bend, every movement
of muscle, the lifting, the rising out
of awareness into the soul of a dream

The bed a raft we paddle with our hands,
each finger an oar that eddies, every wrinkle
a tributary of experience, how light
comes in and essence becomes—the entering,
the passing through

We know river by sky,
by trees, the cedars waxing the light
We know river by bedrock, by the silt
of memory, we know
by its thaw, the ice dividing and coursing
downstream—an arrowhead of geese
flocking north

I take the salve my neighbor made and
rub my joints, tossing the tin can back in to
the creel, casting again, the rod lighter

Around the bend the line shapes, spools
out, the sky curving in

I see my father downstream
and his father somewhere farther

I come from a line of men
who have dreamed the river,
who have lived the going in

I come, too, from a weave of women,
a net of grandmothers with
a delicate touch and cold shoulders

If I move glacially it's because my blood
thickens and I'm sinking deeper
into the dream

When there's slowness in my speech
it's because my thoughts are quickening
to the river

Dreaming the river
I never want to wake

I speak its name

When I dream the river
I am completely particular, I am whole

The synapses in my brain become
trout moving from dark pocket
to strong current

All my bones float like driftwood
pooled together

Becoming the river
I dream the dream
am all dream

Absolute consciousness
An infinite of sensitivity
A river of horses

As the river
I leave the dream

When I disappear you might notice
a small splash of light, a ripple
in the air, a trembling in the god
of time

If my absence worries you
walk down to the river and you will find
me in every molecule

I'm beyond rivering
when I wake

The entire world quivers

Elegy on How to Return

She steals the fraying lace of fog and robes it
over the water. Lights hang from limbs
of trees, the forest wired celestial. The flame within

timber throws shadows and saints chip stones
from their ancestors' wells. Rain bites river,

millions of flies blister its waterskin.
Indian chiefs dancing on the ridge, pines backlit
by the crescent wrenching moon. Swallows courtship:

a feather. Canoe: one person with paddle,
their silhouette a winged totem, another person

traces clouds while treading water. Nearby
roams a school of moose, and the woman
in the canoe paddles her initials on the watery paper

while the sun inks temporary tattoos on the shoreline.
If you ever come looking for this place

keep fast between the mountains and meadow, listen
for the sound of rain, and allow the distances to vanish.
When you catch your breath

make sure it's limitless, that the sky ponders every option
for where to turn it.

Notes and Additional Acknowledgments

The epigraph in "Voyaging" is borrowed from James Galvin's poem "Hematite Lake" from *God's Mistress*.

Also in "Voyaging" there is mention of Anathallo. They were a band and "Genesserat" a song from their album *Floating World*.

The epigraph in "Sundial" is borrowed from Li-Young Lee's poem "Our River Now" from *Book of My Nights*.

The epigraph in "A Day at Large" is borrowed from Li-Young Lee's poem "Pillow" also from *Book of My Nights*.

The epigraph in "Claiming" is borrowed from Greg Rappleye, from his book *Holding Down the Earth*.

"Chronicle" gestures to Haruki Murakami—wishing his characters' lost cats all the best.

"Consciousness" nods to Jeffrey Niemeier—pilot, violinist, botanist, man of many hats.

For my parents, each of you, who shall forever know,
and so will I, who exactly you are and what you have given me.

Haybah, it's a dream come true to be bridging this river together. I love rubbing against the merciless and tender Earth with you. My crazy old heart is yours.

Joshua, I am lucky to have you as a big brother, asking the difficult questions, and showing me one way through.

A line of gratitude spooling out to Dan Gerber, David James Duncan, Laura Kasischke, Li-Young Lee, and Michael Delp for singing this book's praises—each of you upstream, clearing fallen branches.

To Tom Hymn, myth and mythmaker, seeker of visions and songwriter extraordinaire: I am grateful for all the early magic.

Jenn Meade, you know I dig your eye for aesthetics and am stoked by how this book looks. Thank you for giving it the right outfit.

Jeff Kraus, I value how you see the dimensions and noise of solitude, where many of these poems where born out of. Thank you for bringing my poems into paint.

Leagues and leagues of thanks and fruitful nights sleep to Kyle Vandevener, Josh Weston, Robert Fanning, Patricia Fargnoli, Chris Dombrowski, Diane DeCillis, John Rybicki, Dennis Hinrichsen, Russ Thorburn, Rob Haight, Jack Ridl, and Donald Hall for your conversations and comments on my work. Endless gleaming things from the river I hold out to each of you. My writing is more prismatic thanks to you.

The life and work of **Z.G. Tomaszewski** is the mold of a confidence that is fragile and learned. A spiritual wavering of breath exhaled, a dream cross-hatched through memory. Tomaszewski's writings often burrow in fields swiftly gone, a glimpse of terrain captured, with impulse to keep moving.

www.ingramcontent.com/pod-product-compliance
Lightning Source LLC
LaVergne TN
LVHW041508070426
835507LV00012B/1408